HOW TO
TAKE
OF YOU

Advice from the Ancestors,
edited and updated for
MODERN LIVING

A
RETROMETRO
TECHNOBOOK

Published by CL Leavey & Co,
A3 The Green Business Centre
Stanford Bridge, Worcestershire WR6 6SA

Copyright © 2012 Claire Leavey
First published 2012

Retro Metro Technobooks No.1
ISBN 978-0-9570768-0-8

Claire Leavey is hereby identified as the author of this
work in accordance with Section 77 of the Copyright,
Designs and Patents Act 1988.

British Library Cataloguing in Publication Data. A catalogue
record for this book is available from the British Library.

Printed in Great Britain by
Orphans Press, Leominster

Set throughout in Gill Sans,
first used on a shopfront by Eric Gill in 1926

Cover illustration taken from an
American lead printer's plate mounted
on a hardwood block, C.1915.

www.retrometro.co

CONTENTS

HOW TO
TAKE CARE
OF YOUR CLOTHES

FOREWORD

FOR SO MANY years, clothing has been so cheap — and credit so easily available — that no-one has really felt the need to take care of anything but their very best garments. And so rarely has there been the need to clean these special items, that the job has usually been handed to the nearest dry-cleaning specialist without a qualm for the expense.

It's sad to note that this has resulted in the loss of a huge amount of valuable knowledge, and now, as prices begin to rise once more to the point where a new garment becomes a treat rather than a weekly expectation, many of us are casting about for information on how to keep precious clothing in good condition for years, if not decades — and finding very little to go on.

For this reason, I have put together this, the first of what I hope will become a series of 'Retro Metro Technobooks'. The contents are principally drawn from old books which I have collected over the years, and most of those I have used to compile this volume date from early Victorian times to the 1950s. I have tested much of the information, and in the sections on machine washing and hand laundry have added much of my own. Other information, such as that concerning removal of stains from brown shoes and straw hats, or the use of ivy juice to renovate worn clothes, is taken straight from the page without examination.

For this reason, please exercise your own caution and judgment when trying any of the more unusual recommendations in this book – and when deciding whether it's safe to handwash a given "dry clean only" garment, or whether you should stick to sponging. And, as ever, "if in doubt, read the instructions"!

There is now no doubt that the days of the shoddily-made single-wear garment are over, at least for a generation or so. With the help of this book, I'm certain that you'll soon find you enjoy taking good care of your favourite pieces as much as you once enjoyed shopping for new ones.

Claire Leavey,
October 2011

1: STORAGE HINTS AND TIPS

Storage Space
Ample storage space is a first hand requisite for the best care of clothing; it should provide for an orderly arrangement in chests, closets, or drawers. The closet should be fitted with a rod to hold hangers, which placed side by side make for an economy of space. Closets filled with clothing need frequent airing.

Covers
Garments which hang for any length of time should have covers. The material for these should not be too heavy, but close enough in weave to keep out the dust. There are various types of covers, some opening down the front, which makes it a very simple matter to take out garments or put them away. Others have a flap which buttons up at the bottom. This is very good when the garment will hang for a long time, as there is no chance for dust to get into the garment from the floor of the closet.

Other covers for protective storage are made of paper lined with cedar; others are coated with moth-proof substances. Plastic covers are commonly available too. You can make your own covers using the pattern shown in Chapter 8, and then increase the moth protection by using herbal repellent products inside them.

Additional Storage
If the storage space is limited, there are bed boxes (long, shallow boxes, sometimes on castors so they

can roll easily under the bed); these can be long enough to take a garment full length. Portable closets, made of heavy cloth supported by a wood or iron frame, may be had, too.

Care in Putting Clothes into Store

Garments should never be put away when soiled; some stains, if not removed, will deepen in colour and be found indelible when the garment is taken out. Soiled garments are more likely to be attacked by moths than those that are fresh and clean, since it is the traces of dirt, perspiration, skin and food left on the clothes that the grubs will feed on as they hatch and grow. Careful cleaning and wrapping are actually better protection than repellents.

Plenty of coat hangers should be provided, so that garments, slips and negligees may all have their own places.

Care should be taken that garments do not become wrinkled, stretched or change colour when stored. Suits, shirts, coats and dresses are better cared for if hung, but should be covered. If it is necessary to fold any garment, try to have the folds like those into which the garment falls when in use. Dainty coloured garments may fade unless stored in the dark, and white garments if covered with dark blue tissue paper seem less likely to turn yellow.

Protection from Moths

Clothes moths will attack any fabric of animal origin, namely: furs, woollens, cashmere and silks, and these are rendered particularly appetising if they aren't completely clean when stored. Cottons, linens and synthetics are safe. Constant vigilance is needed to keep your expensive woollens and silks safe, with an annual emptying and cleaning out of the wardrobe the most effective means of nipping infestations in the bud.

Old wardrobes and chests often used to be made entirely of aromatic cedar wood, since this is found offensive by moths and other insect life, and will even kill young larvae if the wood is fresh. Sand the inner surfaces of old cedar drawers to revive the scent, or put a few drops of Moth Oil on the wood before renewing drawer liners. Keeping clothes well covered while in store, cleaning them properly before putting away, and ensuring that the storage is kept tightly closed when not deliberately opened for airing, will go a long way towards keeping moths at bay. The aroma of cedar, or rosemary, lavender, artemesia, or strongly scented old geraniums, will all serve to ward off any moths looking for a new home. Ready-blended Moth Oil is a convenient and pleasing repellent mixture.

To be perfectly sure that your clothes are safe from moth attack, and to keep your wardrobe smelling sweet, all woollen, silken, fur and cashmere items should be aired in the sunshine every spring, and brushed thoroughly while outside. While you leave your garments hanging all about the orchard trees, the wardrobe and drawers should be carefully swept or vacuumed out to remove all trace of fluff and lint, where moth eggs might be lurking. While you work, any evidence of moth attack will be quickly spotted, and the fresh air and sunshine will see off anything living.

There are numerous chemical moth-killing papers, bags and gadgets to be had, but these seem to irritate the sensitive lining of the nose until they are too weak to be useful! By far the best remedy is protection – so follow careful wardrobe hygiene, and use aromatic oils to persuade any passing moths that they would be happier somewhere else!

Hats

Hats should be thoroughly brushed when put away for the season, each hat in a separate box, if space permits, packed with tissue paper.

Shelves should be placed in the upper part of the cupboard, the lower one within reach, for the storage of hats in daily use. The upper shelves may be used for the storage of hats not in use for the season.

Shoes

Shoe boxes may be built on the floor of closets if there is height enough to place the rod so garments will not rest on the box. Shoe bags which protect the shoes from dust, or shoe racks which hold the shoes by the heel, may be fastened to the cupboard door. There should be an ample supply of shoe trees.

2: PROPER CARE PAYS FOR ITSELF

Think Before you Wash!

There is no need to thrust every garment into the washing machine as soon as you have used it once. These simple guidelines should minimise your laundry bill:

Clothing once worn should be at least shaken, or better, brushed and aired before hanging in the cupboard. Shoes should be dusted and trees placed in them as soon as they are removed, in order to preserve the shape.

Garments should be pressed as often as seems necessary to keep the wearer well groomed. Spots should be removed as soon as discovered, the process depending upon the nature of the spot and the material 'spotted'. Biobar Super Household Soap will remove most marks and stains, ammonia and washing soda are also useful. See the chapter on laundry, 'Wise Words from a Washerwoman', starting on p14.

Pay swift attention to the repair of small rips and tears, to sewing on buttons which have become loosened, replacing lost snap fasteners, and reattaching bits of trimming. Attending to these little jobs will save time in the end, and often embarrassment.

All dust and dirt should be brushed from all outer clothing as soon as it is removed. Woollen and silk garments may be brushed; also hats. Various types of brushes are ideal for this purpose: short bristle brushes for woollen material; a whisk broom for any general brushing, and a soft bristled brush for silk and velvet. It is well to keep a scrap of velvet at hand for brushing the dust from silk or satin hats and dresses.

Underclothing and hosiery should never be allowed to become so soiled that much soap and hard rubbing are necessary to clean them. Blood stains, fresh or dried, may be removed completely by treating with Biobar Super Soap before machine washing. Sheer stockings should be washed after each wearing, for two reasons: washing removes perspiration and grit which injure the fibre, and also changes the places where the strain in wearing comes. To quickly hand-wash tights in the evening, simply rub the feet onto a dampened Biobar and squeeze the soap through the fabric in a basin of warm water before rinsing out and hanging to drip dry.

Pressing garments at home is a great saving of expense if one does not have to consider the element of time consumed in the process. The work of pressing would be much lightened if the items listed on page 24 were a part of the worker's equipment. Careful pressing is as necessary a process in the successful making of a garment as are careful cutting and careful stitching. It blends the seams together and gives to the whole a trim tailored finish. It is also the secret weapon in keeping clothes looking as though they had just been made when wearing them during the years to come ...

Care of Woollen Clothing

Brush thoroughly and with the nap if the cloth has such a surface. Shake after brushing to remove the dirt. The edges of tucks should be turned back, and pockets turned inside out, to remove lint. The vacuum cleaner, using a suitable attachment, and with the suction turned low if this is possible, is a great tool for keeping woollen garments clean and smart without even the trouble of sponging.

Remove all spots, whether by the use of a little plain water, powdered chalk, fuller's earth, or spot remover such as Biobar Super Household Soap.

Darn the tears in woollen garments with threads of wool, not cotton or polyester.

Pilling (the development of little balls where the clothing has been rubbed) occurs in fine, soft woollens. Coarser, more durable woollens will not suffer. Light pilling may be removed using a purpose-made electric machine, while a 'comb' bearing a coarse abrasive strip is more effective on larger pills, and over larger areas too. Sometimes, on felted items for example, huge pills develop, and these may only be tackled by carefully shearing through the strings of fibre beneath the clumps with sharp scissors or a razor blade.

Care of Silk Clothing

Brush carefully with velvet or soft brush. Remove spots. Fuller's Earth (plain) is one of the best absorbents of grease. A little sprinkled on a grease spot and left for a time will remove the grease as will be found when the earth is brushed off. If the spot has other matter than grease, it may be necessary to make further trials with water or something stronger.

Washable silks should be washed in suds of a neutral white soap and lukewarm or cold water, wrapped tightly in a bath towel to absorb the moisture, and ironed immediately.

Wrinkles may be removed from silk dresses by hanging them over the steam from a bath-tub filled with hot water. Be careful that there is not enough moisture rising to settle into the folds of the material and make it positively wet.

Care of Cottons and Linens

Brushing rubs the dirt into the fibre of cotton or linen, therefore washing is the best procedure. Do not press white cotton garments too often as they are apt to turn yellow.

3: WISE WORDS FROM A WASHERWOMAN

Spot Cleaning is Spot on!

There is no need to machine-wash an entire garment every time it suffers a splash of ketchup, coffee or curry. Keep at hand a small bowl, sponge, pieces of absorbent rag to use as blotters, Biobar Super Soap (and maybe ammonia for really bad marks), and simply sponge off stains and blotches before they cause embarrassment - or worse, set into permanent stains. Lighter marks can be removed while the garment is still being worn. More serious marks will need attention at the sink.

Use a blunt knife to scrape off any solid material such as chocolate or tar, or any dollops of fallen sauce, before moistening your sponge with cold water and rubbing it onto the Biobar to pick up a good amount of soap. Use this to gently massage out the mark, then rinse the sponge in clean water before again massaging the fabric to remove the soap, along with any remaining traces of the soiling material. Gently squeezing the affected area in a clean, dry towel will dry it out to such an extent that the garment will then be ready for anything else the day might throw at it!

Efficient and Effective Machine Washing

The first thing you can do to minimise the expense of laundry is to only ever run a washing machine with a full load. Too often the temptation is to wash a couple of favourite items because they are needed quickly. This is simply flushing money down the drain!

The second useful thing to remember is that soft water (in former times rain water was prized for the purpose) washes clothes most effectively, and enables you to use a minimal amount of soap or detergent. The addition of a tablespoon of borax to the powder drawer should allow you to reduce the amount of expensive detergent per wash by at least half. In hard water areas, add two spoonsful.

Avoid the convenience of ready-made single dose detergent tablets or sachets of liquid. These satanic inventions give the detergent manufacturer complete control over the amount of detergent used per wash – and the manufacturer, scenting the advantage, will of course be inclined to generosity in this, if not in price!

The less detergent you can get away with using, the more money will be saved – and the longer your clothes will last, into the bargain! Some people are experimenting with washing their clothes with no detergent at all, and this with surprisingly good effects. In this case, spot-cleaning stains, collars and cuffs before washing of course becomes essential, and using alternatives to laundry detergent such as soap nuts and eco-balls will do very good work. If you are keen to take this purist route, and particularly if you intend to wash at the lowest possible temperatures, matters will be greatly helped if you add a tablespoonful or two of borax to the powder drawer in order to soften the water as it passes through the machine. The borax will also help to combat bad smells - and to be extra sure of a satisfactory wash, four or five drops of essential oil of lavender or rosemary will eliminate any remaining smells or bacteria.

Cottons and linens which are principally used close to the skin or hair (this also including bedlinen and towels) will inevitably pick up a certain amount of the grease which naturally exudes from the body, this mingled with a certain amount of ground-in dirt. When washing such items, it is possible to keep both the detergent dosage and the temperature of the wash to a minimum by programming a pre-wash, and adding a cupful of washing soda (sodium carbonate) in the pre-wash section of the powder drawer. The soda should easily rinse the grease quite out before the machine proceeds to the main stage of the wash. Avoid using soda on coloured items, however, since it will slowly bleach out the colour over time.

Spots of dirt, grass and mud smears, fruit juice splashes, grimy cuffs and collars are best prepared for the laundry by moistening and rubbing with Biobar Super Household Soap. Once the Biobar is well into the grain of the fabric, the garment may be left in the basket for as long as is needed before being thrown into the machine and washed to a state of perfect cleanliness in the usual way.

Out of Condition

There is absolutely no practical need for any the fabric 'conditioners' which inventive manufacturers have persuaded people to add to their rinsing waters these days. Not only do they actually achieve the impression of enhanced softness by breaking down the fibres and so shortening the life of your clothes, they also coat the fibres with substances which inhibit the absorbency of natural fabrics, so rendering towels and cotton undergarments far less suited to their intended purpose. They also serve to irritate the skin of sensitive individuals, and so are certainly not to be used on garments intended for small children, invalids or babies.

Bad Smells

The plague of bad smells of perspiration, mustiness etc, remaining in the wash even after items have been laundered and dried has given rise to the addition of almost unbearably strong perfumes to most of the proprietary detergents, fabric 'conditioners' etc. These certainly give the impression of luxury – but serve only to mask smells, not to remove them, as anyone who has had a nasty shock when first applying the iron to a well-loved shirt will know too well. Add four or five drops of essential oil of lavender to the laundry powder in the drawer, and you will find that the unpleasant lingering of 'body odour' becomes a thing of the past. Adding borax too will help.

A sour, musty aroma in dried laundry results from two failings: first, taking too long to get the wet clothes hung out; and second, drying clothes too slowly in a windless indoor environment. Both these can be solved by good management.

Speedy and Effective Drying

There is no doubt that drying laundered items outdoors in the fresh air is by far the best choice. The sunshine will make whites whiter, will help kill the microbes which perpetuate bad smells, and by means of its heat will dry the clothes off quickly. A good breeze will not only help the clothes to dry even faster, but will also gently beat them as they hang, softening them to the touch without damage, and imparting a fresh, delicious fragrance that no manufacturer's so-called 'conditioner' could ever hope to match. Line drying is also essential if your house is at all prone to dampness.

If you have no choice but to dry your clothes indoors, invest in a suspended clothes airer of the Victorian kind. Choose a warm location, such as near the cooker or fireplace, if speed is essential, or position the airer over the bath if you plan to use it very much in drying woollens. By so hanging the clothes high in the living space, you expose them to considerably improved air movement, and also to marginally higher temperatures. This is all the result of convection, by which means warm air rises up to the ceiling, and then, as it cools, circulates back down the walls until it is warmed and rises once again.

This is a marvellously effective means of drying clothes, even on wet days, when a slightly open window will be all you need to aid speedy drying. A little heat in the room (even from a tiny electric heater) will also greatly enhance the effect, simply by causing the air to move around more quickly. Unless you are struggling to keep a large family clad with no access to an outdoor line, there is simply no need for the expense of a tumble drier.

Why Iron?

As a wise matriarch might once have said, the iron was

invented by men for flattening women. There is simply no need to iron bedding, kitchen teatowels, or casual clothing if these are folded carefully and piled in the drawer or cupboard for a sufficiently long time before use. This is precisely what we once used linen presses for. There is certainly no need to iron stretchy modern undergarments, since any wrinkles disappear as soon as you put them on! There is certainly a case to be made for ironing work shirts and those fine linen garments reserved for best – but in most cases, a good shake out and a blow on the line should do much of this work for you in any event. Pure linens should be removed from the line just before they are quite dry, and this will greatly ease the job of ironing them.

Starching is a Help, not a Hindrance

Another useful tip is that a weak solution of hot water starch, once used, will keep woven cottons and linens subtly smoothed and stiffened for the duration of several washes without ironing (subject to careful folding, as above) – and will noticeably help them to repel the dirt in between times, too.

Nothing is more vile to the proper washer-woman than those strangely-scented cans of spray starch used at the point of ironing. Thankfully, good hot-water starch can still be obtained via the internet, and is made up at a rate of about a dessertspoonful to a pint of water. Add a little cold water to the powder in a saucepan, and mix the starch to a paste before gradually diluting up to the full pint. Half a teaspoonful of borax added to the starching solution will greatly enhance the brightness of whites. Boil thoroughly, stirring all the while, for a minute or two, and then transfer to the sink and dilute down with cold water to a volume suitable for immersing the items to be treated.

It is really no extra trouble to make up the solution if a whole load of washing for starching is laundered at one time. Starching should be done to freshly washed items before they are dried. On work shirts, it may be preferred to dip only the collars and cuffs into the solution and leave the rest of the fabric unstarched. Once starched, the garments should be well wrung (a quick spin in the machine is the easiest way to expel surplus solution), and the items should then be well shaken out before hanging, and collected for ironing (if you must) when still barely damp.

4: DRY CLEAN ONLY?

Hand-wash, Sponge and Press for Less!

The instruction to dry-clean items is often put there by manufacturers purely as a precaution to protect special garments against careless and ignorant laundry. In fact, you'll sometimes find that the English language label instructions tell you to dry clean while those in French give instructions for a careful cold or cool hand wash! The chic French know how to care for fine fabrics in a way we have simply lost.

Handwashing Woollens

By woollens, we tend to mean all materials of animal origin, so including cashmere, angora, mohair and silks. A deep flat-bottomed Belfast sink is by far the best for handwashing, and for so many other tasks. Bear this in mind for the next time you remodel your kitchen! Prepare a lukewarm, cool or even cold washing solution using a proprietary liquid wool wash, or by sprinkling a small handful of flaked white laundry soap into a little very hot water, leaving it for ten minutes or so to dissolve, and then adjusting the temperature down to the required level by adding cold.

Add a dash of ammonia for very dirty woollens as long as they aren't black (it may spoil the colour), or to restore the colour of faded silks. You could also add a little borax in the washing water to aid the cleansing action of the soap, and this will also help to guard against shrinkage. Lay the garment as flat as possible in the bottom of the sink, and gently squeeze the soapy water through it before leaving to soak for ten minutes to half an hour. Return to the sink and squeeze through more thoroughly, but again without rubbing, agitating, or excessively swishing the garment about. Run the water out, and then rinse thoroughly using cold water.

A splash of white vinegar in the first rinsing water will purge soap residue beautifully, further enhancing the body and softness. A tablespoon of methylated spirits in the last rinsing water imparts a lovely smooth gloss and enhanced body to silks. Gently press out most of the surplus water, then roll any particularly delicate garments up in a towel, squeezing gently to remove as much of the remaining water as possible, and then lay over an airer or similar, pulling the garment back into shape, and then leave it to dry flat. Stockings and tights, and any sturdier woollen items, may be hung to drip dry without too much ceremony.

Woven Woollens

If you follow the instructions given above, you may well find you can hand-wash a number of woven woollen garments too. However, many expensive woven garments such as tweed jackets and woollen trousers cannot be washed in the usual way because they have interfacings which might be spoilt by the agitation of washing, or because their fibres will shrink and mat if immersed in even cold water. These garments are prime subjects for 'sponging'.

I.   Lay the garment flat on an ironing board or tabletop, or hang against the back of a door.

2. Spot clean as required using Biobar Super Soap on a damp sponge.

3. Prepare a sponging solution in a small bowl: you can choose either a lukewarm woolwash or soap solution (see under 'knitted items', above), or a solution of household ammonia. Ammonia is an ideal choice for more thorough cleaning of really dirty tweeds and flannels. Soak a hard natural sponge or lintless cloth with the solution and squeeze out well, then gently rub over the surface of the garment, following the direction of the fabric's nap or grain, squeezing out in the solution repeatedly as you work to keep the sponge clean.

4. Repeat using clean cold water, rinsing the sponge out frequently, and change the water as required until it remains clear.

5. Turn the garment over, and sponge the reverse as per steps 2 to 4.

6. Press according to the instructions given in Chapter 5, spritz over to fragrance with Lavender Essence if desired, and then air.

5: PRESSING QUESTIONS

Equipment for Pressing

The most important items you'll need for pressing are a cloth and an iron. A pressing cloth should be of some fast colour, better a white material, lintless, and free from all dressing (ie: well washed before using). Old muslin or cheesecloth are both very good. Streaked and blotchy effects are caused by pressing material under a heavy cloth which cannot be uniformly dampened, or if it has dressing in it or is very closely woven.

Small daubers made of a small piece of soft cloth are more convenient to use and more satisfactory than the corner of the regular pressing cloth, to moisten seams, to shrink out fullness, and for use wherever moisture is best applied, intermittently, in small amounts and in local spots.

Tissue paper is very satisfactory to press silks and other sheer materials under. A hotter iron can be used, and no moisture is necessary. Never press directly onto the material.

The ironing board should be well padded, clean, and smooth as for ironing, The stand on which it is supported should be well built and substantial, holding the board steady. It should be of such a height that one does not have to stoop unnecessarily nor feel as if reaching up when pressing. The board should be of the regulation length and width, tapering at one end so that a skirt may be slipped easily over it. Sleeve seams may be pressed open over a sleeve board, or by using a rolling pin or neckless bottle wrapped up in a thick layer of cloth.

The iron should be kept smooth with paraffin and wiped clean before using. A pan of water kept near at hand is a convenience.

How to Press

Press all nap materials with and not against the nap. Steam fabrics with a distinct pile by holding the back of the material near an upright hot iron over which a cloth wrung from water has been stretched, or in front of an upright automatic steam iron if you have one. The seams are worked open from the under side to prevent finger-prints on the right side, After the velvet has been steamed, brush it with the nap and stretch the material with the pile surface up, on a smooth surface, single fold, until thoroughly dry.

Pressing is not Ironing

Too much emphasis cannot be put on this point. Pressing is done with a moderately hot iron, over tissue or over a moist or dry pressing cloth, by lifting the iron over the material, with the pressure applied locally. Ironing is done directly on the material with a hot iron, using backward and forward strokes, the combination of heat and pressure on the already moistened article bringing out the texture and character of the piece. Texture and character will only be lost, however, when clothes are wrongly pressed. Ironing restores the texture and finish of laundered materials, while careful pressing retains them.

Pressing in the Sewing Room

You will find that your finished garments obtain a professional level of polish if you follow these simple rules for pressing as you construct them:

- All new materials should be pressed and freed of all wrinkles and the fold crease before laying the pattern. The crease is sometimes very stubborn and almost impossible to get out after the garment is assembled, without losing its shape.

- Remodelling vintage items: it is important that all old seams, pleats, gathers, marks made by stitching, etc., are steamed and pressed out before any constructive step in the remaking is begun.

- Press each seam before it joins another, with a moderately hot iron, by lifting the iron over the material and feeling your way with the point of the iron rather than taking a stroke as in ironing.

- All seams are pressed open first, even if later they are to be finished together. For example, press open the seams in double collars and cuffs, etc., before turning to the right side, and you will find that it makes a sharper, flatter edge, and better corners may be had. Armhole seams are first pressed open and all the fullness shrunk out of them before any edge finish is applied.

- All darts in underarm seams are pressed up,

and the seams and darts in sleeves are pressed open.

- Hems too are pressed flat in cotton and cloth garments, but not in silks, chiffons, and other similar lightweight fabrics, which should be pressed very stingily all the way through.

- Pressing may be made a very valuable shortcut and time saver in the sewing room. 'Centre front', 'centre back', and other temporary lines may be indicated by a pressed line rather than by running a basting or chalk line, etc.

- A thorough pressing should be the final step in the finishing of any garment.

6: ACCESSORIES
AFTER THE FACT

Care of Leather Shoes

Shoes should be carefully brushed and free from dust; patent kid shoes should be wiped with a soft cloth to remove dust, and occasionally have petroleum jelly or Apis Hide Food rubbed into them to keep them soft and pliable, and prevent cracking. All leather shoes should be kept on trees when not being worn, as this will keep them in shape much better.

Always protect leather shoes from rainy weather, because frequent wetting not only injures the leather, but puts the shoes badly out of shape. In the past people used overshoes, known as 'rubbers', which went on over their shoes to keep them dry in wet weather. If caught in a rain-storm and the shoes become wet, do not dry them very near the fire as this has a tendency to destroy the leather, making it dry and crack. Dry the shoes well away from artificial heat sources, and speed up the process by stuffing them with crumpled newspaper. Change this as often as necessary as it soaks up the moisture. It is best as soon as the shoes dry off, to rub petroleum jelly or Apis Hide Food into them to soften the leather. Attending to the proper care of the shoes will ensure twice the length of service that can otherwise be expected.

White tide-marks which appear on brown leather shoes when they have been exposed to sea water can be removed by dissolving half a teaspoon of washing soda in two tablespoons of hot milk. Clean the shoes all over with this preparation, allow to dry thoroughly, and afterwards polish with a good brown polish. The marks should have disappeared.

Stains on brown leather boots and shoes can be removed by dissolving about half a teaspoonful of citric acid in a cup of water and rubbing them all over with a sponge. Dry off and then polish.

Before storing leather boots and shoes for any length of time, it is a good idea to wipe them over with essential oil of lavender, as this will prevent the development of mildew or mould.

It is an economy to keep more than one pair of shoes going at a time, as the alternate wearing permits the shaping of the shoe by the trees when they are not being worn.

Keep shoes repaired as long as it is advisable. Worn-down heels, aside from the untidy appearance, help to spoil the shape of the shoe, and will even tire you out faster by stressing your posture. When having them repaired, full soles and heels are better than half soles because they keep the shoes in shape longer.

Care of Satin Shoes

To clean satin shoes, take a clean lintless rag, dip into methylated spirits, and rub the shoes over, following the grain of the satin. Change to a clean piece of cloth as soon as it becomes dirty. Pale satin shoes that get beyond cleaning can be dyed a darker shade with coloured ink. Pour a little ink into a saucer, make a dauber with a bunched-up soft cotton rag, and use this to apply the ink evenly.

Care of Suede Shoes

Stuff the shoes full of soft paper, then clean with a little turpentine applied on a clean lintless rag. Keep on rubbing and turning the rag until the shoes look clean.

Remove grease marks by sprinkling with French chalk, then roll in a towel and leave for several days. Brush off the powder, and you should find the marks have gone. If you are short of time, rub marks away with fine emery cloth, a fine emery board, or fine sandpaper.

Care of Good Hats

A hat very soon betrays the lack of care by its owner. It should be carefully brushed, and bits of trimming which have been loosened by the wind should be tacked into place and perked up. Use a piece of velvet to wipe dust from silk or satin hats. Straw hats may be wiped quickly with a piece of cloth dipped in alcohol.

If a velvet or silk hat has been caught in a sudden shower, hang it over a stove or radiator, being careful to keep it in shape and not let it touch anything which would mark the covering.

Felt hats can be cleaned with a flannel or sponge dipped in ammonia and hot water.

White straw hats can be cleaned very successfully with hydrogen peroxide. Use an old toothbrush and rub the peroxide well in. Sponge over carefully with cold water and then dry in the open air. It will become very white again.

Black straw hats can be renovated by rubbing in a small quantity of olive oil. Rub in with a small brush and leave to dry for two or three days. After this, rub the hat over with tissue paper to remove any excess.

Millinery ribbon can be successfully cleaned with methylated spirit, then carefully ironed.

Care of Gloves

Put gloves away in pairs; long narrow boxes are best for this purpose. Woollen gloves should be protected from moths by close covering and inclusion of some aromatic cedar etc inside the box.

Kid and other fine leather gloves should be drawn from the hands, never pulled off by the tips. Inflate the fingers when the glove has been drawn off, and pull the fingers into shape.

Washable kid gloves may be cleaned by putting them on the hands and washing them in lukewarm suds made with neutral white soap. Rinse them thoroughly and dry them slowly.

Silk gloves may be turned wrong side out to remove them. Cotton gloves stand harder wear than kid or silk. Wash silk gloves in cold or lukewarm water, and with a neutral white soap.

Care of Silk and Wool Scarves

Silk and wool scarves should be carefully hand-washed in cold or lukewarm water, and with a neutral white soap, according to the instructions given on pages 21-22. Store silk and wool scarves inside plastic bags or closely covered boxes inside drawers or wardrobe, only once freshly washed and carefully folded. Include some aromatic cedar, rosemary, lavender etc inside the bag or box to further guard against moths.

Care of Tights and Stockings

Silk and nylon stockings should always be washed before being worn. Woollen stockings should be washed in a warm soapy lather, rinsed and dried as quickly as possible, but away from direct heat.

Sheer nylon and silk stockings should be washed after each wearing, for two reasons: washing removes perspiration and grit which injure the fibre, and also changes the places where the strain in wearing comes. Hot water should never be used, but rather wash gently in a warm soapy lather to which a little white vinegar has been added, and then rinse well. Dry away from direct heat, ideally hanging to drip from a suspended airer. There is no need to risk ironing knitted silk or nylon.

To quickly hand-wash sheer nylon tights in the evening, simply rub the wetted feet onto a moistened Biobar and squeeze the soap through the fabric in a basin of warm water before rinsing out and hanging to drip dry overnight.

7: A STITCH IN TIME SAVES NINE

Mend Your Ways!
Timely mending is your first defence against the ruination of your favourite clothes. Repair all rips immediately. Many glove dealers and department stores will mend torn places for a small sum and often replace catches without charge. Most areas have at least one alteration specialist, and they will usually carry out repairs according to a clear scale of charges. Better still, though, quickly and easily make small repairs yourself without leaving home – and at no charge!

A Handy Mending Kit
A well-stocked mending basket, always at hand, should contain the following: pincushion (full of pins and needles and the needles threaded with different coloured silks and cottons for emergency repairs); hooks and eyes; snap fasteners; buttons, sewing thread (cotton and silk), tapes, small bits of cotton, linen, wool, silk for patching, darning cotton, mending tissue, scissors, thimble, needles, pins, a 'quick unpick', and an emery for removing marks from suede etc.

Renewing Worn Shirts and Blouses
Thin or worn patches in clothing can be covered with new pieces which are cut, finished and attached to the garment so as to make the piece look as though it were part of the original pattern. A good tip, suitable for blouses which are worn under the arms, is to set

on a section of material in such a way as to make it appear that it was part of the original pattern. Mark out first of all the shape of the yoke on the blouse with tack stitches. The dart seam may give the direction for this. Sleeve, side, and shoulder seams are unpicked so that the new section (which should be cut, allowing for turnings, with the old section as a pattern) may be tacked on. The yoke is best edge-stitched on and all the seams are then closed. The back section can be renewed in the same way, if necessary, and a decorative scallop will give the new piece such a flourish that no-one will ever suspect!

A work shirt's collar, once worn through on the fold where the fabric rubs against the neck, may be removed and replaced on the garment the other way out. Use your quick unpick to carefully break through the stitches and the repair will be quite invisible.

Shiny Patches on Well-worn Clothing
Shiny patches can be dealt with by means of a tea made from the juice of ivy leaves. Wash the leaves, cover with cold water, boil gently til tender, leave until cold and then strain for use. Wear rubber gloves when working with ivy.

Patching Woven Fabrics
Wear, and damage to flat areas of a garment such as rips and holes, can be repaired using a set-in patch, and, if you do it carefully enough, on certain fabrics the damage will be rendered quite invisible. If you have made the garment yourself, you have no doubt had the good sense to keep a few scraps of fabric aside for precisely

this purpose. With a shop-bought garment, sadly, this option is not open to us. All is not lost, however!

It is often possible to use a little of the turned-up fabric from a hem, or perhaps to steal a good-sized piece from the inside of a pocket, always replacing the stolen fabric with a patch of some other material, so that the good functioning and long life of the cannibalised area are maintained.

The patches must always be set in on a straight thread and the corners must be worked absolutely cleanly, so that in certain weaves and patterns the join is not visible at all. Make sure your patch extends well over the damaged part, or your work will be almost thrown away. If patching woollen flannel material, there is no need to turn under and hem the edges of the repair, but a careful herring-bone stitch all round will suffice.

Left: The material is cut out in a square or rectangle all round the worn or torn place and the patch cut to fit, adding double the width of the seam and the turn-in, ie: $^3/5^{th}$ in. (1.5 cm) must be allowed. The corners of the cut-out hole must be nicked by $^1/5^{th}$ in. (3 mm) or so, so that the edge of the material can give.

Right: The outer edge of the patch is turned under, and hemmed over on the machine or stitched down. Here it is being oversewn by hand. NB: Contrasting thread is only being used here to make the picture clearer!

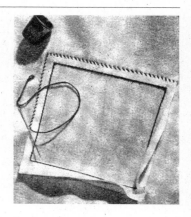

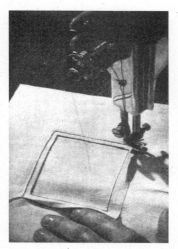

Left: Here the patch is being hemmed down by machine. In order to obtain particularly clean and neat corner seams, leave the needle in the material when turning it to work another edge.

Right: Once the patch has been fully stitched into place, the edges of the original fabric on the reverse are nicked in the corners, turned under, and hand-stitched down, giving a very neat and durable finish on both sides of the repair.

Patching non-woven fabrics

Patch torn leather, PVC or vinyl items on the reverse using a small piece of strong cotton or linen cloth, glued into place with a flexible PVA, clear UHU type, or contact adhesive. Use the unpicker to slit a seam in the lining if necessary, place the leather flat, face down, on a strong, non-printed plastic bag, tease the edges of the tear together as closely as possible, apply an even layer of glue over the area to be patched, and press the patch down firmly onto the glued area, maintaining pressure until the patch is firmly attached.

Turn the garment over as soon as possible, carefully remove bag, and check that no surplus glue has leaked onto the exterior. Wipe off surplus PVA with a damp cloth, or scrape other types of glue away with a blade. If the patch shows through any remaining hole, touch it in with coloured ink or a colour-matched mix of acrylic paint. Resew any broken lining seams by hand.

Darning

Darning is a thoroughly useful skill which will not only resurrect many favourites once they are worn to the point where they would ordinarily join the rag box, but it also makes economic sense of buying the very finest, most expensive – and warmest – woollen socks! Darning can be performed on both knitted and woven fabrics, and is most conveniently tackled when the place has just about worn thin, rather than when it has sprung a gaping hole.

A few words will explain how to darn a thin place. Be sure that the cotton or wool you use is of the proper thickness; never have it too coarse for the stuff. It s even well sometimes to darn with some of the ravellings drawn from what is to be mended. Always use wool to darn wool, since other yarns will not have sufficient give for the mend to hang right. And on a knitted woollen fabric, such as a sock or jersey, it is as well to stretch the fabric over one of those wooden eggs or mushrooms specially made for the purpose.

Darning should be done on the wrong side, thus: Work backwards and forwards making rows of even stitches – picking up and leaving an even number of threads, or taking up one and leaving two – until the thin place is well covered. Then work across for the second row, picking up the darning thread only. Should there be an actual hole, whether in a knitted fabric or too small to patch, threads must be taken right across for the first row, and in the second row these threads will be alternately picked up and passed over.

And finally, remember: keeping supplies at hand, and making repairs promptly, will keep the wearing apparel above reproach.

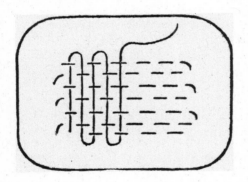

8: TWO USEFUL PATTERNS

Old sheets and duvet covers make a good source of fabric for the shoe bag and moth protection clothes cover shown here. For the shoe bag you will also need 180cm (2 yards) of half-inch cotton tape, and for the cover you will need either four buttons or some velcro. Allow at least 2.5 cm or 1" for hems and seams.

To Make a Hanging Cover

Fold the fabric in two, measure and chalk out the two pattern pieces along the fold as shown opposite, using the length of the garment to be covered to determine the length of the cover's front. Open out the fabric and hem between the two snip marks at the top on each piece, and from the two snip marks to the bottom at each side of the back. Fold where marked at the bottom of each piece, hem down so fabric is double, and either add buttons and button holes at the positions shown or attach velcro. Sew the two pieces right sides together, and turn right way out. Feed garment on hanger into cover, and the hook will emerge through the hole at the top.

To Make a Shoe Bag

Measure and chalk out pattern as shown. If you shorten it a little, two bags will fit side by side across a 150cm width fabric remnant. Snip where shown and hem outward from snips to ends, then fold over the 4cm and hem down to make tube in which drawstring will run. Fold right sides together at centre line, sew up to the snip marks, and turn right way out. Cut the tape in half and thread each piece through both sides of the tube from opposite ends, knotting to join each into a drawstring loop.

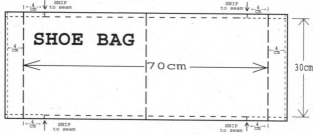

40

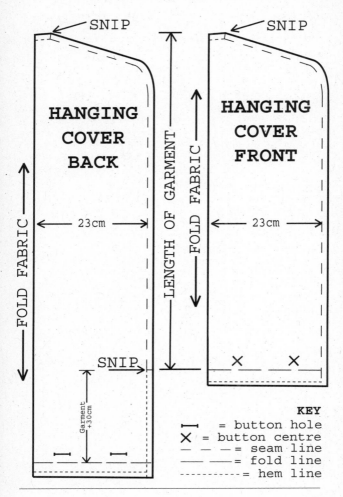

SNIP

SNIP

HANGING
COVER
BACK

HANGING
COVER
FRONT

FOLD FABRIC

LENGTH OF GARMENT

FOLD FABRIC

23cm

23cm

SNIP

Garment +30cm

X   X

KEY

⊢▬⊣ = button hole

✕ = button centre

— — — = seam line

———— = fold line

---------- = hem line

GLOSSARY

Ammonia

Chemical name: ammonium hydroxide. Ammonia is a compound of nitrogen and hydrogen, with an eye-wateringly pungent aroma, and a moderately alkaline cleansing action. It is generated by decomposing organic material, and was at one time produced industrially by distilling the hooves and horns of slaughtered animals, hence its former name 'spirit of hartshorn'. Never combine with chlorine bleach since this produces a highly explosive gas and poisons. Known to be strongly antiseptic since 1895, it is an irritant to humans (though completely non-toxic), and care should be observed in any disposal since it is lethal to aquatic life. Household ammonia is generally supplied at a dilution of 5–10% in water. Excellent for loosening dirt from woollens, and essential in sponging.

Borax

Chemical name: sodium tetraborate decahydrate. Borax is a salt of boracic acid, found in many countries of Asia and in America, as a kind of saline crust on the shores of certain lakes. It is purified for use by means of caustic soda. Elsewhere, Borax 'substitute' is manufactured from boracic acid, carbonate of soda, etc. Powdered borax is used in washing, and its action is to help soften the water, and to bleach the linen. It is supposed to be much less injurious to linen than most other preparations used for the same purpose, and is kind to the hands.

Citric Acid

Chemical name: 3-carboxy-3-hydroxypentanedioic acid. A mild, naturally derived acid obtained in crystal form. Used to remove limescale from household appliances, it is also to be found in many green household cleaning products such as loo and surface cleaners. Also used to cause minerals to fall out from hard water (chelation), so softening water and aiding the actions of soaps and other cleansers. Can be used to remove salty tide marks from water-damaged clothing.

Daubers

Daubers are little bunches of lintless rag, with a flat layer of the fabric used to hold the scrunched-up material inside a ball shape. Used for dying, pressing etc.

Eco-balls

Eco-balls are an intriguing manufactured gadget consisting of three balls which are placed in the drum of the washing machine. They work by ionising the oxygen molecules in the water, so enhancing its natural solvent power. Thanks to their unique action, Eco-balls are effective at any temperature, enhance the softening action of the washing machine on the clothes, and because nothing is added to the water, they are ideal for those with very sensitive skin. The manufacturers claim that each set of Eco-balls may be used up to one thousand times before replacement.

Fabric Conditioner

Also called fabric softener. Sold in the form of liquid, crystals, or sheets for use in the tumble drier, conditioners coat the fibres at the molecular level with a thin layer of chemical lubricant to give the illusion of softness, plus hydrophobic (water repellent) and electrically charged chemicals designed to counteract the static electricity which develops in tumble-dried synthetic fibres. Some manufacturers also claim that their products make clothes dry faster, increase stain resistance, and speed ironing. Natural fabrics don't develop static cling, and in any event, for this and for 'softening', a cupful of white vinegar will do a better, safer job. First developed during the early 20th century to counteract the rough texture which cotton developed when subject to artificial drying, early conditioners coated fabrics with olive oil, corn oil or tallow (animal fat), emulsified with soap. Modern fabric conditioners are usually based on quaternary ammonium salts, antimicrobially active substances which are also found in antiseptics and spermicides. Thankfully, their antimicrobial properties are rendered inactive by soaps, some detergents, hard water, and by cotton fibres – but they are still generally held to be irritant, and have been blamed for a wide range of allergic reactions, ranging from mild skin and respiratory irritation, right up to death caused by anaphylaxis. Quaternium-15, a salt commonly used in conditioners, is the single most often found cause of allergic contact dermatitis on the hands.

A huge number of other chemicals are also added to conditioners, many of which are entirely unnecessary for any given fabric, and so represent money literally flushed away. As the usefulness of these products has become increasingly questionable, manufacturers have focused on fragrancing to maintaining sales (and prices), and in recent years they have even been moved to modify their manufacturing technology purely in order to cram previously undreamt-of quantities of perfume into the products, so increasing the potential irritant risk.

Never use conditioner on towels, cotton underwear or washable nappies, since it will destroy their absorbency. Never use on microfibre fabrics. And never pour fabric conditioner directly onto any fabrics, even in dilution, since this may cause permanent marking. Always wear gloves.

Hydrogen peroxide

Hydrogen peroxide is a weakly acid oxygen bleach and cleansing agent, commonly available from pharmacies in dilutions of 3 and 6%. Notwithstanding its impressive cleansing properties, in low concentrations it biodegrades into harmless water and oxygen. This makes it an increasingly popular alternative for chlorine bleaches, even in industrial applications.

Laundry detergent

Whether in powder or liquid form, laundry detergents are complex mixtures of water softeners, surfactants, bleach, enzymes, brighteners, fragrances, and many other agents. Some of the materials included, such as the bleaches and water softeners (or 'buffers'), can be mildly caustic and so shorten the life of clothes. The principal active ingredients are called 'surfactants', and are very useful in helping to loosen the dirt. There are anionic, cationic and ionic surfactants, these names deriving from the electrical charge of the molecules in the substance in question. Surfactants work because they are 'amphiphilic', that is to say, partly hydrophilic (loving water) and partly hydrophobic (hating water). This means that they partly cling to the water molecules and partly cling to anything that isn't water – ie the grease and dirt lying on the surface of your dirty clothes. Used in moderation, they are ideal for machine washing, but are these days somewhat over-used, and do their part in making linens less durable. Some plant-derived surfactants are biodegradable, while others, of petrochemical origin, are not.

Pilling

Where balls of clumped fibres appear on the surface of a garment as a result of rubbing during wearing. May be picked, snipped or shaved away.

Quick unpick

A 'quick unpick' is an invaluable gadget in the mending toolkit. It is a slender steel implement with an unequal fork shape at its head. The inside edge of the fork shape is sharpened to make a cutting blade, and while one end is blunted completely, the longer has a sharp piercing point. This gadget makes light work of breaking into seams without damaging the fabric, although of course a little care is recommended to prevent disasters. They can be readily obtained from any department store or haberdasher's.

Soap

Chemical name: sodium (or potassium) palmate, cocoate, tallowate, olivate, etc, depending on the oil or fat used to make it. Soap is manufactured from oil, tallow, or some other form of fat, and a preparation of soda, or lye, or alkali as it is called. Soap is remarkable for its solubility, and is therefore readily dissolved in water. It works by readily mixing with the dirt and the grease in dirty clothes, thereby rendering them also soluble. Soap is an emulsifying salt, and used soap in waste water biodegrades readily.

Soap nuts

Botanical name: Sapindus Mukorossi. Soapnuts come from Northern India and Nepal, and are the dried husks of the fruit of a wild tree. Containing 12 to 18% natural soap compounds (saponins), they provide a gentle but effective dirt-lifting action without the use of any artificial substances, or the use of energy in their manufacture. The trees live and produce for ninety years or so, and the soap nuts can be reused several times and then composted. Soapnuts are generally placed in a cotton drawstring bag inside the drum of an automatic washing machine, then hung up to dry between washes. Despite a high purchase price, they have a reputation for being the cheapest means of machine-washing clothes principally thanks to the opportunity for repeated re-use.

Washing soda

Chemical name: sodium carbonate. Soda is prepared by a chemical process from sea or common salt (sodium chloride) and certain acids. The two substances are so combined that a proper alkali is produced. Like soap, soda owes its usefulness to its great solubility and solvent power. For very dirty or greasy things it is indispensable. Always rinse thoroughly out of white clothes or they will discolour. Never use it on woollen items for it raises the platelets on the fibres and so will coarsen them and cause matting. Keep absolutely dry in use or the powder will set into a solid block inside the jar. Wear gloves when handling soda.

THE END

HOW TO RUN
A THRIFTY KITCHEN

RETROMETRO
TECHNOBOOK
No. 2

COMING
OCTOBER
2012

More advice
from the Ancestors,
edited and updated for
MODERN LIVING
ISBN 978-0-9570768-1-5

Goodbye stains, hello ...

BIOBAR ®

SUPER *household* SOAP

☞ OBTAIN SUPPLIES FROM RETROMETRO.CO – DO NOT RISK DELAY ☜

REPEL THE INVADER
WITH

THE STILL

MOTH OIL

MOTH OIL

A natural blend of pure plant oils.
Repels only insects, not humans!